Workbook Two
Of the Business Essentials Series

GETTING YOUR FINANCIALS RIGHT

JOHN MILLAR

Copyright © 2016 John Millar

All rights reserved. No part of this publication may be reproduced, distributed, or transmitted in any form or by any means, including photocopying, recording, or other electronic or mechanical methods, without the prior written permission of the publisher, except in the case of brief quotations embodied in critical reviews and certain other noncommercial uses permitted by copyright law

All rights reserved.

ISBN-10:1533140499
ISBN-13:9781533140494

DEDICATION

I dedicate this book to my mother and father, who raised me while self-employed. They taught me to work hard and listen to everyone but to make my own choices as to what is right and what is wrong.. and oh, did I mention work hard?

Anyone who tells you to work smart not hard hasn't ever done it tough and realized that if you work smart AND hard you will achieve more than you can possibly dream.

CONTENTS

	Dedication	i
1	Product Description	Pg 6
2	Workbook Content	Pg 7
3	Financial Ratios and Quality Indicators	Pg 40
3	7 Steps to More Profit in Less Time	Pg 47
4	The Business Essentials Series	Pg 50
5	About the Author	Pg 53
6	Client Testimonial	Pg 55

To Your Success!

PRODUCT DESCRIPTION

GETTING YOUR FINANCIALS RIGHT

This is the core of it all isn't it? What's the point of working yourself into a frenzy week-in-week-out when the financials are spiraling out of control? In this very important DVD we look at the ways in which business can gain control and undertake good financial management.

If you want your business to grow profitably and reliably then this is a must have DVD. Getting your finances in order is a mature and reasonable response to owning and operating a business. You never know, a small re-direction of energies and goals may make all the difference. For many of our clients, the repetition of non-productive tasks meant they were sabotaging their own success. A few well learned and informative tips from this DVD have helped them turn their businesses around.

Good financial management is essential for the expansion of your business. Getting your finances in order means your business can work more efficiently and puts you in a better position when seeking funding for growth.

Improving your financial situation

Getting your business back on financial track may involve a number of steps – but how do you know which are the right steps for your business?

- Do you need to seek professional advice?
- Do you need to introduce new financial systems?
- Does your staff need re-training in more efficient methods?

Whatever the case, this DVD and the consultants at More Profit Less Time will assist you in deciding upon the best remediation methods that are applicable to your situation.

You can make cash flow and budgeting work for you. Discover how in this DVD.

Obtaining additional finance

Obtaining finance is often the next crucial step in business growth. An up-to-date business plan outlining new goals and objectives will ensure you are well prepared when seeking finance. There are various sources of finance options available including savings, investors and government grants. To take full advantage of your options you need to be financially organised and prepared.

In this easy-to-follow and powerful business DVD:

• You will learn the importance of understanding your financials by intelligent use of budgets, plans, forecasts and outcomes. You are the one responsible for the progress of your business. Why not be responsible for its growth, development and profitability?
• Become the best friend of your accountant and book-keepers by being more financially literate. Knowing what questions to ask to improve your situation is just as important as knowing how to

run your business. Being in control financially is not just about tax compliance. It's about knowing what action to take under what circumstances. And learning about your options and alternatives via this DVD is a very intelligent choice.

Includes 1 DVD Video, 1 CD Audio and Printed PDF Workbook.

To purchase this module go to our website www.moreprofitlesstime.com.

I believe that businesses have a right, a duty and an obligation to achieve three things.

> They must make profit, they must improve cash flow and they must create a saleable asset.

> If you are not achieving all those three things then you are not achieving your

---

> Most business owners I have met have learned to discount before they can count

---

> Don't Discount

> Why should you actually stop discounting?

> By discounting a little you have to do so much more work to have the same amount of dollars in the bank!

And you discount your price by:

Your sales would have to INCREASE by the amount shown below to keep the same margin…

	20%	25%	30%	35%	40%	45%	50%	55%	60%
2%	11%	9%	7%	6%	5%	5%	4%	4%	3%
4%	25%	19%	15%	13%	11%	10%	9%	8%	7%
6%	43%	32%	25%	21%	18%	15%	14%	12%	11%
8%	67%	47%	36%	30%	25%	22%	19%	17%	15%
10%	100%	67%	50%	40%	33%	29%	25%	22%	20%
12%	150%	92%	67%	52%	43%	36%	32%	28%	25%
14%	233%	127%	88%	67%	54%	45%	39%	34%	30%
16%	400%	178%	114%	84%	67%	55%	47%	41%	36%
18%	900%	257%	150%	106%	82%	67%	56%	49%	53%
20%	-	400%	200%	133%	100%	80%	67%	57%	50%
25%	-	-	500%	250%	167%	125%	100%	83%	71%
30%	-	-	-	600%	300%	200%	150%	120%	100%

The table above indicates the Increase in your sales that are required to compensate for a price discounting strategy. For example, if your margin is 40% and you reduce your price by 10%, you would need your sales volume to increase by 33% to maintain your profit. Rarely has such a strategy worked in the past and it's unlikely it will work in the future…!!

You don't need to discount if you are offering value in your business.

I do advise that you get a really good accountant, bookkeeper, financial planner immediately if you do not already have one.

GETTING YOUR FINANCIALS RIGHT

> You need to know what your profit and loss is, how to use it, what it's all about and where are you going to apply it

> You need to know what your balance sheet is

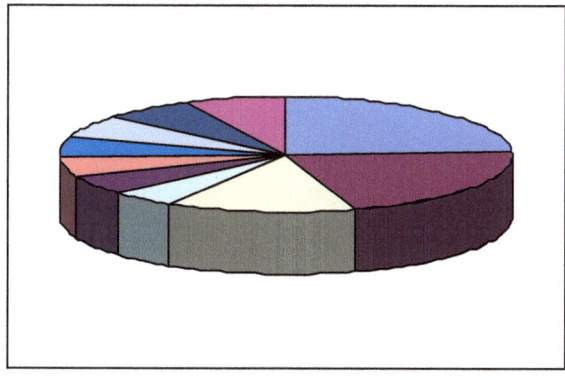

Bridge 21
Balance Sheet
As of January 22, 1999

	Jan 22, '99
ASSETS	
Current Assets	
Checkings / Savings	
Savings, Norwest 50-40106283	156,602.41
KC & Company, 1st United Parker	40,546.59
Bridge21, Norwest 40-40116567	-62,852.71
Petty Cash	116.75
Total Checking/ Savings	134,413.04
Accounts Receivable	
*Accounts Receivable	403,106.59
Total Accounts Receivable	403,106.59
Other Current Assets	
Investment Account	300,000.00
Personal Loans Receivable	3,000.00
Hardware	31,616.11
Software	924.49
Inventory Asset	6,715.41
Due From Employees	36.90
Undeposited Funds	-6,625.00
Total Other Current Assets	333,667.91
Total Current Assets	871,187.54
Other Assets	
Office Equipment	7,676.97
Total Other Assets	7,676.97

You need to know what the breakeven is inside your business

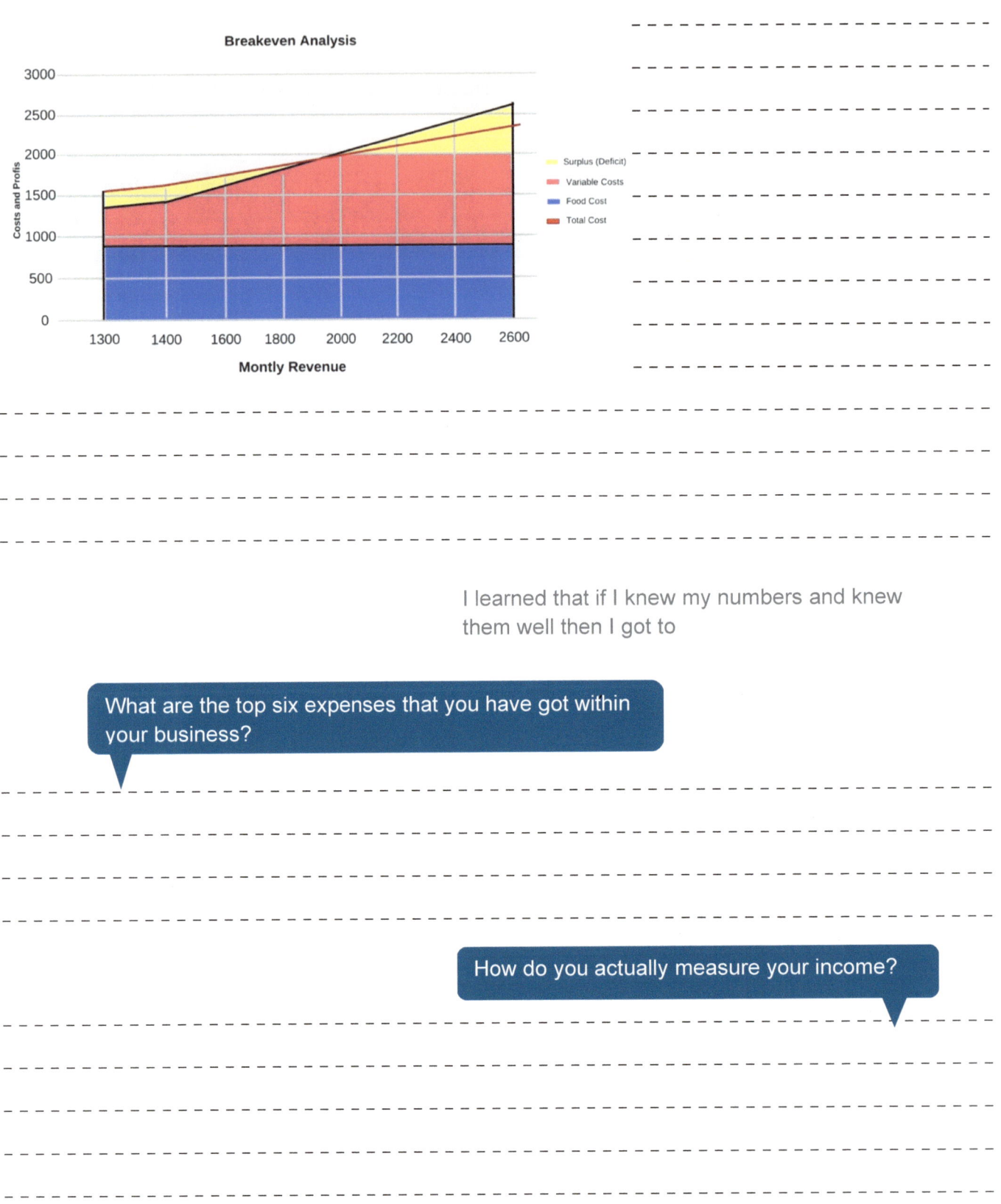

I learned that if I knew my numbers and knew them well then I got to

What are the top six expenses that you have got within your business?

How do you actually measure your income?

> Why do so many potentially great businesses fail in the first year or two OR after being in business for a long time start stagnating and declining?

> First and foremost is lack of quality cash flow

> The next one is no profit.

Wouldn't it be great to have a profitable business that has positive cash flow?

> If you don't have cash flow and you don't have profits you don't have a business

---

If you don't have cash flow and you don't have profits you don't have a business

_____
_____
_____
_____

Do you know what your breakeven point is?

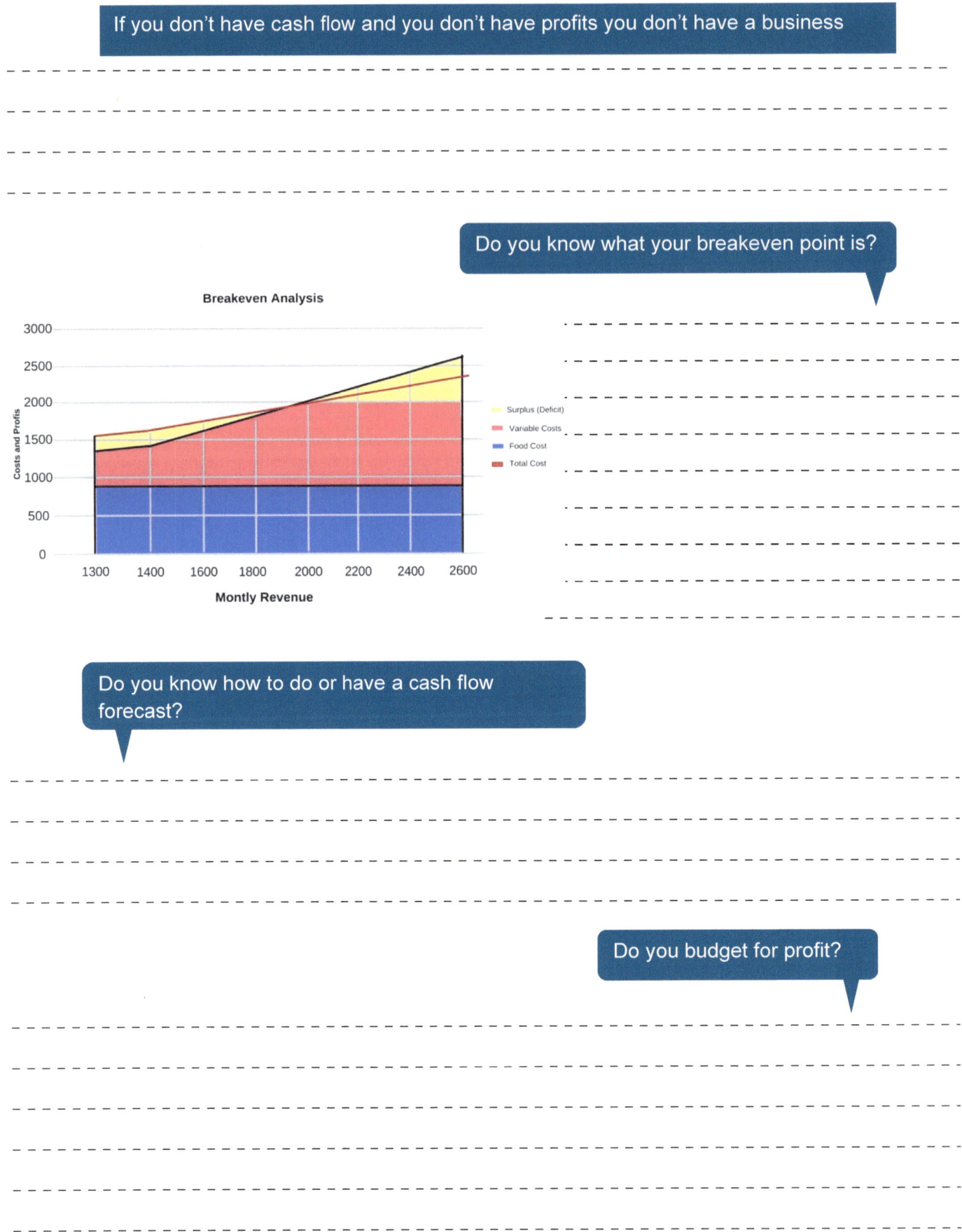

_____
_____
_____
_____
_____
_____

Do you know how to do or have a cash flow forecast?

_____
_____
_____
_____

Do you budget for profit?

_____
_____
_____
_____
_____
_____

Are your books up to date and are they accurate?

Are your financials entered into your accounting software regularly and then reconciled every month?

A good quality accountant will actually help you to make good quality financial business decisions and keep you informed of your progress along the way.

Are you looking at your profit and loss on a monthly basis?

Do you have a system in place that will help you keep on track of where you should actually be financially?

When was the last time you had your accountant and your bookkeeper check your numbers?

Get your financials regularly checked and checked and measured and get checks on your accountant and your bookkeeper making sure that what they are checking is even correct as well.

What is a profit and loss statement?

It records things like your sales, it reports your income, it records things like cost of goods sold.

It also records your gross profit, it records your fixed expenses

> If you don't understand today then find a consultant, a mentor, a bookkeeper, an accountant or all the above and sit down with them and actually go through it all in detail so that you understand it all well enough to start asking intelligent questions and therefore make informed intelligent decisions.

> Total income or sales subtracted by cost of sales and the variable cost gives us our gross profit.

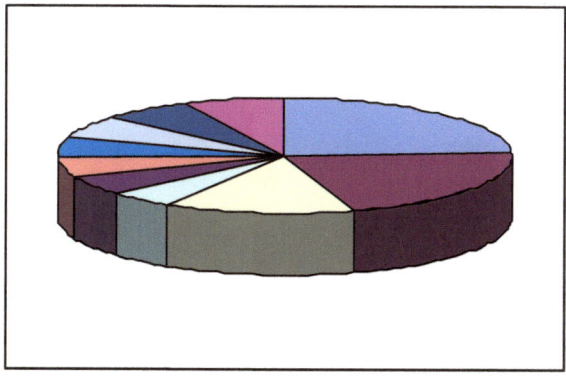

Jan 1 - 22 '99

Expense Summary
Jan 1 – 22, '99

Bridge 21
Balance Sheet
As of January 22, 1999

	Jan 22, '99
ASSETS	
Current Assets	
Checkings / Savings	
Savings, Norwest 50-40106283	156,602.41
KC & Company, 1st United Parker	40,546.59
Bridge21, Norwest 40-40116567	-62,852.71
Petty Cash	116.75
Total Checking/ Savings	134,413.04
Accounts Receivable	
*Accounts Receivable	403,106.59
Total Accounts Receivable	403,106.59
Other Current Assets	
Investment Account	300,000.00
Personal Loans Receivable	3,000.00
Hardware	31,616.11
Software	924.49
Inventory Asset	6,715.41
Due From Employees	36.90
Undeposited Funds	-6,625.00
Total Other Current Assets	333,667.91
Total Current Assets	871,187.54
Other Assets	
Office Equipment	7,676.97
Total Other Assets	7,676.97

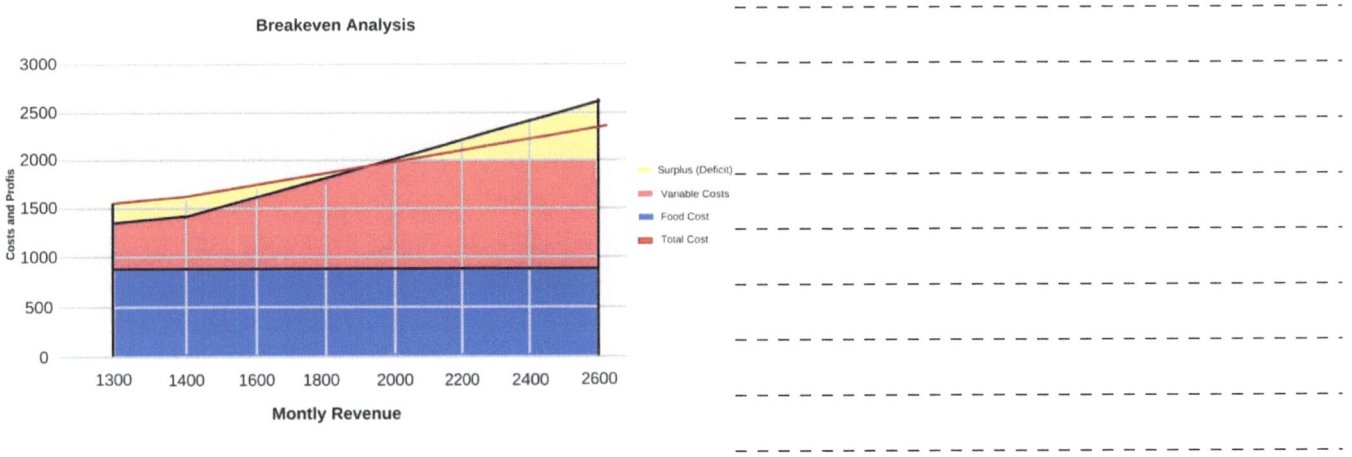

I want you to sit down and actually work out what the gross profit margin is for the blue, the green and the yellow widgets.

The Profit and Loss Statement (P&L)

Records
    Sales / Income
    COGS / COS / Variable
    Gross Profit
    Fixed Expenses
    Net Profit

Here's how it works

Total Income / Sales
-
Cost of Sales / Variables
=
Gross Profit
-
Fixed Expense
=
Net Profit/ (Loss)

XYZ Widget Pty Ltd
Profit and Loss Statement

Sales / Income		
Red Widgets	$	50,000.00
Blue Widgets	$	44,000.00
Green Widgets	$	21,000.00
Yellow Widgets	$	7,000.00
Total Sales	$	-
Cost of Sales		
Red Widgets	$	25,000.00
Blue Widgets	$	15,000.00
Green Widgets	$	17,000.00
Yellow Widgets	$	6,000.00
Total Cost of Sales		63,000.00
Gross Profits	$	59,000.00
Fixed Expense		
Bank Charges	$	2,500.00
Bookkeeping	$	4,100.00
Interest	$	2,200.00
Misc. Expenses	$	1,500.00
Office Supplies	$	3,000.00
Postage	$	1,200.00
Printing & Stationary	$	2,000.00
Rent	$	5,000.00
Sales & Marketing	$	4,000.00
Staff Ammenities	$	800.00
Telephone	$	3,500.00
Wages & Salaries	$	12,000.00
Total Fixed Expense	$	41,800.00
Net Profit/ (loss)	$	17,200.00

> Let's do some numbers…

Firstly, let's work out what our TOTAL Gross Margin Percentage is…

Sales	-	COGS	=	Gross Profits	÷	Total Sales X 100	=	Gross Margin
$122,000	-	$63,000	=	$59,000	÷	$122,000 X 100	=	48.3%

Now let's work out what our HIGHEST Gross Margin product is…For this exercise we will use the same formula, but this time we will do it for each specific product line. We'll start with Red Widgets… First we need to calculate our GROSS PROFIT for Red Widgets…

Red Widgets Sales	-	Red Widgets COGS	=	Our Gross Profits for the Red Widgets
$50,000	-	$25,000	=	$25,000

We can now calculate the Gross Profit margin for our Red Widget Sales…

Sales	-	COGS	=	Gross Profit	÷	Total Sales X 100	=	Gross Margin
$50,000	-	$25,000	=	$25,000	÷	$50,000 X 100	=	50%

> Now it's YOUR turn…
>
> 1. Work out the Gross Profit Margin for Blue, Green & Yellow Widgets…
> 2. What Widget has the highest Gross Margin?
> 3. What Widget has the lowest Gross Margin?

Red Widgets Sales	=	Green Widget	=	Yellow Widget
65.9%	=	19.0%	=	14.2%

> How can you use this information to increase your Net Profit?
> Work out how much extra Net Profit you would make if you had the same amount of total sales and ONLY sold Blue Widgets.

Total Sales	x	Blue Widget Margins	=	Gross Profit	−	Fixed Expenses	=	Net Profit
$122,000	X	65.9%	=	$80,398	−	$41,800	=	$38,598

> **How can you increase your Gross Profit?**
>
> 1. Sell more Higher Margin Goods/Services…
> 2. Re-negotiate with suppliers/Contractors…
> 3. Increase your prices…
>
> **How can you increase your Net Profit?**
>
> 1. Increase Sales…
> 2. Increase your Gross Profit…
> 3. Reduce Fixed Expenses…

The Balance Sheet shows the VALUE and indicates the HEALTH of your business!

ACB Trading CO
Balance Sheet as of Jun 2005

Code	Account			
1-0000	**Assets**			
1-1000	**Current Assets**			
1-1110	Cheque Account	22,546.00		
1-1140	Petty Cash	200.00		
	Total Cash On Hand		22,746.00	
1-1200	Trade Debtors	165,551.00		
1-1210	Less Prov'n for Doubtful Debts	(1,000)		
	Total Accounts Receivable		164,551.00	
1-1300	Inventory	150,000.00		
1-1400	Prepaid Insurance	0.00		
1-1800	Deposit Bond - Rent	5,016.00		
	Total other Current Assets		5,016.00	
	Total Current Assets			342,313.00
1-2000	Fixed Assets			
1-2500	Vehicles			
1-2510	Vehicles - at Cost	73,174.00		
1-2520	Vehicles - Accum Dep	(16,940.00)	56,234.00	
	Total Fixed Assets			56,234.00
	Total Assets			398,547.00
2-0000	Liabilities			
2-1000	Current Liabilities			
2-1200	Trade Creditors	171,897.00		
	Total Trade Creditors		171,897.00	
2-1310	GST Collected	38,122.00		
2-1330	GST Paid	(47,947.00)		
	Total GST Liabilities		(9,825.00)	
2-1410	PAYG Installment	1,882.00		
2-1430	Provision for Annual Leave	3,500.00		
	Total Payroll Liabilities		5,382.00	
	Total Current Liabilities			167,454.00
2-2000	Non Current Liabilities			
2-2050	HP Creditor	25,000.00		
2-2100	Bank Loans	50,000.00		
	Total Non Current Liabilities			75,000.00
	Total Liabilities			242,454.00
	Net Assets			154,093.00
3-0000	Equity			
3-1000	Share holders Equity			
3-1100	Paid up Capital - Ordinary	2.00		
	Total Shareholder Equity		2.00	
3-8000	Retained Earnings	61,245.00		
3-9000	Current Year Earnings	94,846.00		
	Total Retained Earnings		156,091.00	
	Total Equity			156,093.00

How to Calculate your Break Even Point...

It is Vital to your business success to know the number of sales you need to Break

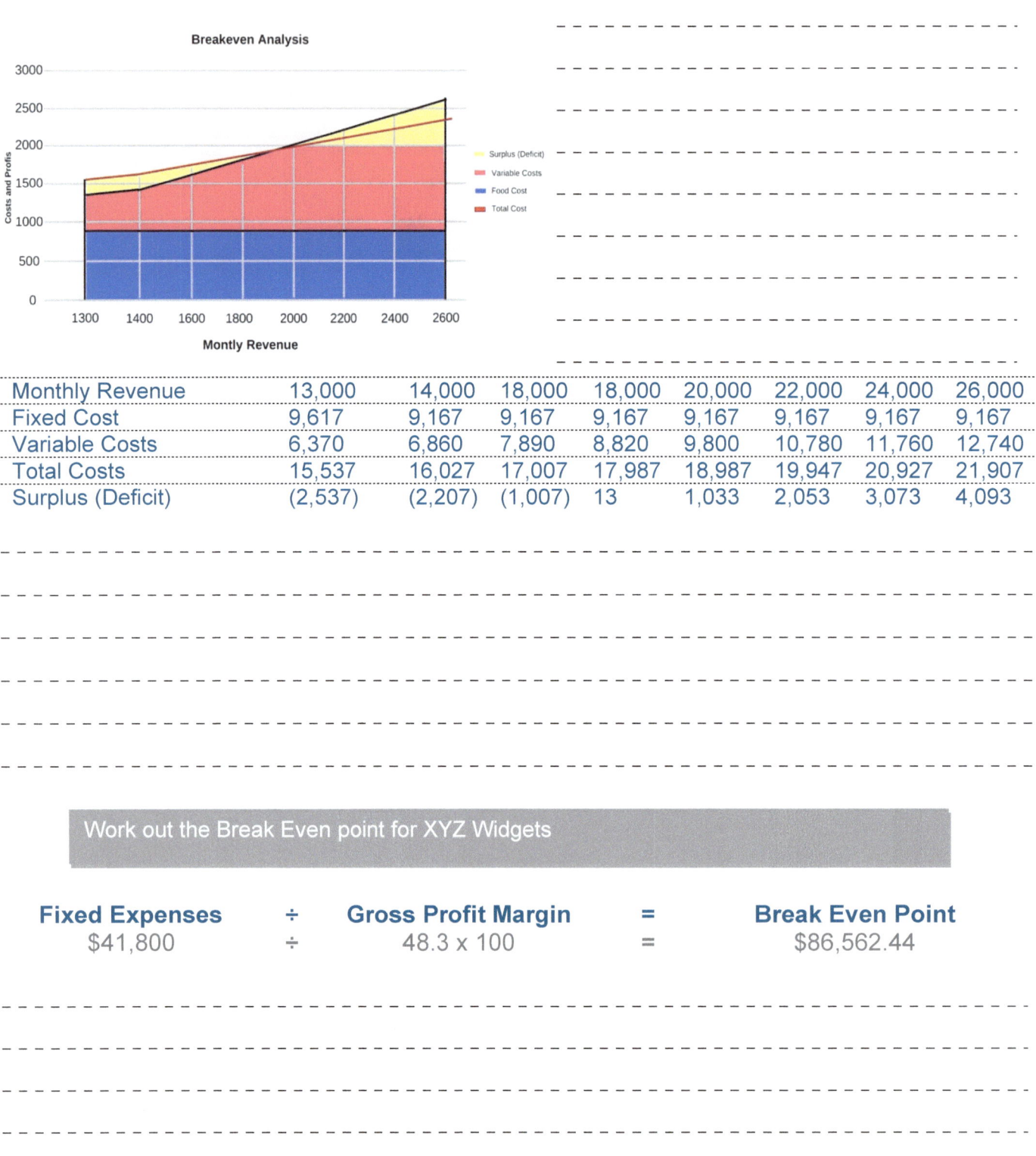

Monthly Revenue	13,000	14,000	18,000	18,000	20,000	22,000	24,000	26,000
Fixed Cost	9,617	9,167	9,167	9,167	9,167	9,167	9,167	9,167
Variable Costs	6,370	6,860	7,890	8,820	9,800	10,780	11,760	12,740
Total Costs	15,537	16,027	17,007	17,987	18,987	19,947	20,927	21,907
Surplus (Deficit)	(2,537)	(2,207)	(1,007)	13	1,033	2,053	3,073	4,093

Work out the Break Even point for XYZ Widgets

Fixed Expenses	÷	**Gross Profit Margin**	=	**Break Even Point**
$41,800	÷	48.3 x 100	=	$86,562.44

GETTING YOUR FINANCIALS RIGHT

What widget has the highest gross margin?

_____
_____
_____
_____

What widget has the lowest gross margin?

_____
_____
_____
_____

How can you use this information to actually increase your Net Profit?

_____
_____
_____
_____

Focus on selling the most profitable products more often.

> Eighty, twenty your products and services down to a level where you understand your numbers as eighty percent of your products are probably only delivering twenty percent of your profit and twenty percent of your products are actually delivering eighty percent of your profit.

_____
_____
_____
_____

Sell much higher margin products and services

Renegotiate with the suppliers and contractors

Increase your prices

You can lose a substantial amount of clients by increasing your prices by just 10% before you actually bank less money

---

And you increase your price by:
Your sales would have to DECLINE by the amount shown before your Profit is reduced

	20%	25%	30%	35%	40%	45%	50%	55%	60%
2%	9%	7%	6%	5%	5%	4%	4%	4%	3%
4%	17%	14%	12%	10%	9%	8%	7%	7%	6%
6%	23%	19%	17%	15%	13%	12%	11%	10%	9%
8%	29%	24%	21%	19%	17%	15%	14%	13%	12%
10%	33%	29%	25%	22%	20%	18%	17%	15%	14%
12%	38%	32%	29%	26%	23%	21%	19%	18%	17%
14%	41%	36%	32%	29%	26%	24%	22%	20%	19%
16%	44%	39%	35%	31%	29%	26%	24%	23%	21%
18%	47%	42%	38%	34%	31%	29%	26%	25%	23%
20%	50%	44%	40%	36%	33%	31%	29%	27%	25%
25%	56%	50%	45%	42%	38%	36%	33%	31%	29%
30%	60%	55%	50%	46%	43%	40%	38%	35%	33%

When you adopt a premium pricing strategy this table shows the amount by which your sales would have to decline following a price increase before your gross profit is reduced below its current level. For example, at the same 40% margin, a 10% increase in your price could sustain a 20% reduction in sales volume.

Make sure that you are asking a premium for premium products and you are adding real value into your services

----

How can you increase your net profit?

You can increase your sales

You can increase your gross profit

You can reduce fixed expenses.

You can't cost cut your way to a magnificent business

> Reduce your basic expenses but don't do so at the detriment of being able to offer excellent services, which will allow you to increase sales and increase profit.

The balance sheet records some very basic things.

It looks at your assets and your liabilities

It looks at the equity that you have within your business

The value of your business

It shows the health of your business.

The assets within your balance sheet are the things that you are actually own.

The liabilities within your balance sheet are the things that you owe.

There are two main types of assets.

Current assets are assets that can be basically converted into cash. They are things like bank accounts, debtors and perhaps some stock that might actually be easily convertible into cash.

Fixed assets and those things that have a longer life span and are not easily converted into cash like machine or capital equipment, vehicles, buildings

Your balance sheet also then looks at your liabilities (both long and short term)

Equity is the total assets less the total liabilities

The balance sheet shows you the value and indicates the health of your business.

Go back and going through your individual expenses

What are the things that are going to provide value to your business?

What are the things that are going to provide value to your clients?

Anything else that you can't honestly say adds value in those areas are pimping your business.

Breakeven is the point after which you now make profit

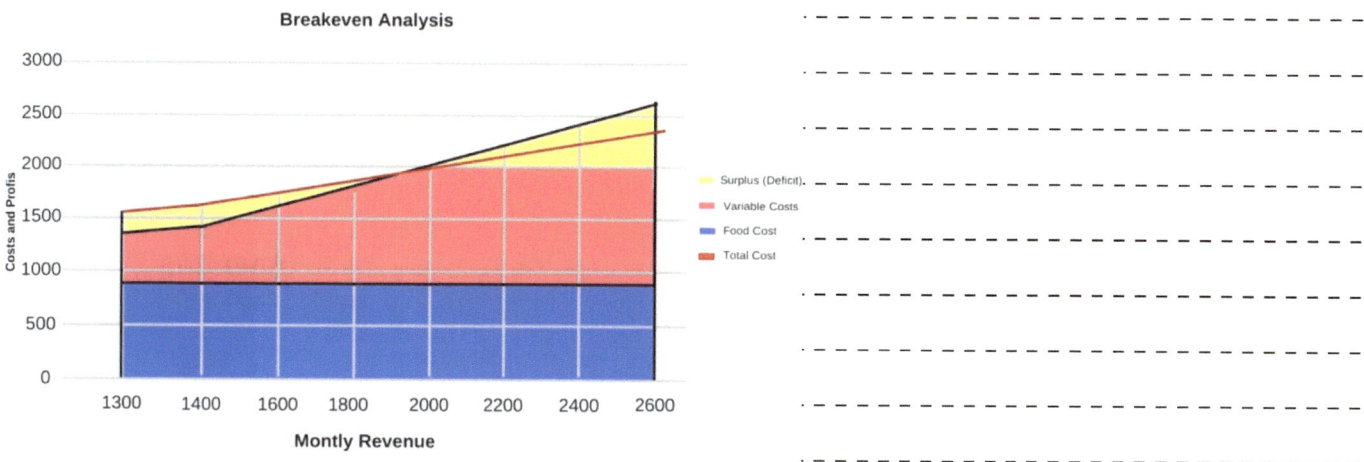

Monthly Revenue	13,000	14,000	18,000	18,000	20,000	22,000	24,000	26,000
Fixed Cost	9,167	9,167	9,167	9,167	9,167	9,167	9,167	9,167
Variable Costs	6,370	6,860	7,840	8,820	9,800	10,780	11,760	12,740
Total Costs	15,537	16,027	17,007	17,987	18,987	19,947	20,927	21,907
Surplus Deficit	(2,537)	(2,207)	(1,007)	13	1,033	2,053	3,073	4,093

Fixed expenses, divided by your gross profit margins multiplied by a hundred equals a breakeven point.

Calculate the break even for yourself inside your business.

Do you understand your P&L and balance sheet and then how can I actually forecast the cash flow.

Cash only moves in a circular direction.

CASH INFLOWS
(sales and receipts)

CASH OUTFLOWS
(paying expenses)

_____
_____
_____
_____
_____

Record your spending habits.

What is your cash on hand?

_____
_____
_____
_____
_____

What are your loan repayments, incoming cash and outgoing cash?

_____
_____
_____
_____
_____

What are your loan repayments, incoming cash and outgoing cash?

Sit with your accountant or book keeper and do a cash flow forecast.

Look at four different main cash sources.

- Income that's generated by the business
- Borrowed cash
- Sale of assets
- Capital injection

Make sure that you are using your cash in your business for general expenses, making

sure that you are profitable, with enough there for the purchase of fixed assets and the purchase of stock.

It is also very important to manage all of our creditors to make sure that you have paid in full and on time

Make sure you have allocated sufficient funds and planned for one of the most important part in the use of cash which is owners drawings or wages.

Make sure that you balanced your bank statement every month.

Knowing your cash gap is very important

A cash gap is the difference between the amount of money that you have coming in compared to the amount of money going out.

The Cash Gap – An Easily Visualised Concept

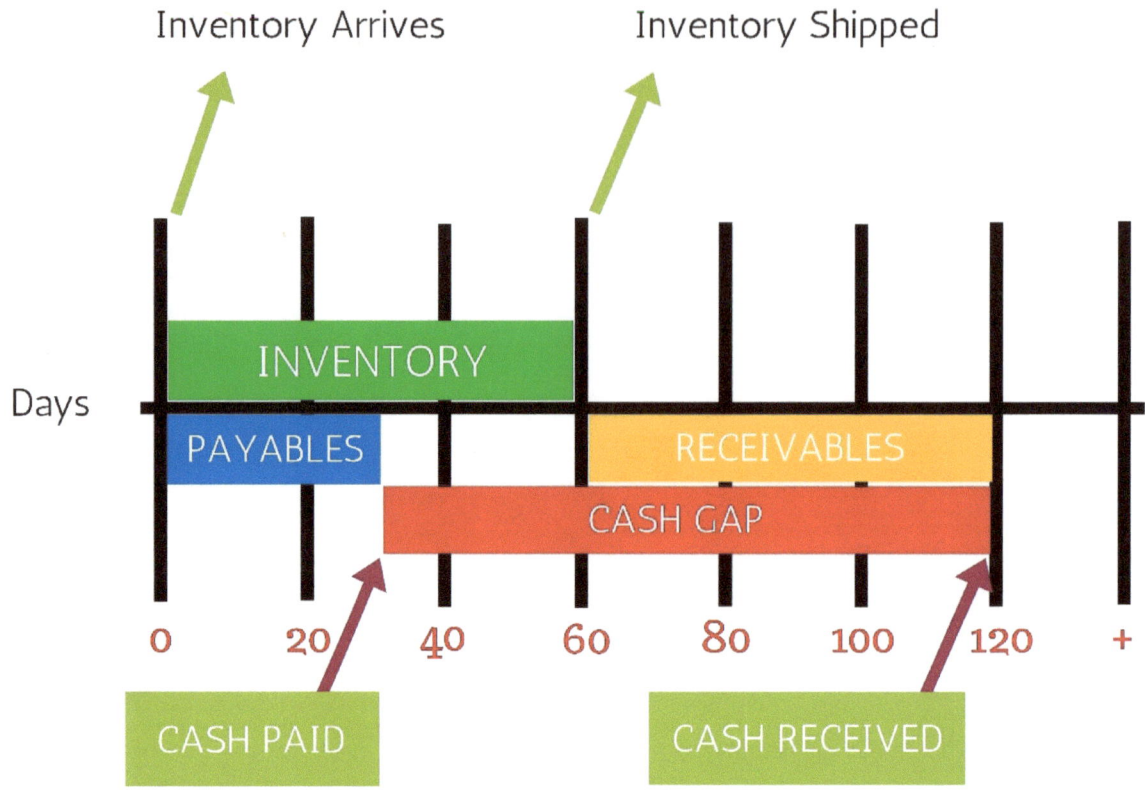

The green within the cash debt represents the days of an inventory, the blue are the days of the payables. The yellow is when we actually.

Use the widgets for example.

If I have to order an inventory that needs to last maybe for thirty days but I am on a fourteen day account. The reality is that by the time I have ordered it I then have the payables where I have to pay for within fourteen days. I have then got stock that's going to last me fourteen days beyond that. Then I have already paid for this and my customers haven't purchased it. Let's assume that my customers are on a thirty-day account. From day one all the way through to the end Iam not getting paid for another thirty days for the last of that stock until its actually being invoiced.

Can you get longer trading terms, can you offer shorter trading terms, can you take part payments and deposits?

What are the strategies that you can actually do to reduce that cash gap into your favor?

There is only three ways to reduce your cash gap

First of all you must increase the account payables period

In other words how long it takes before you need to pay for it.

Secondly decrease collection period

Collect money faster

Are you offering terms to new clients that haven't earned the terms yet?

Reduce or eliminate most credit terms whenever possible

Have you given them longer terms than what they deserve?

Don't let other people use your business as an interest free line of credit.

Make sure that you adjust your business to suit so that you can remain cash flow positive and profitable.

If you are offering value plus you have a unique selling proposition and guarantee it will make it easier to be able to receive and give the appropriate terms that you need for a positive cash gap.

A budget is essentially a target or a goal for a business.

Do you know how much profit your business needs or are simply hoping to breakeven which means you are probably budgeting to make a loss!

You need a budget for your sales

_____
_____
_____
_____

You need to have a budget for the cost of goods sold

_____
_____
_____
_____

You need to have a budget for your expenses

_____
_____
_____
_____

You MUST budget for your planned profit.

_____
_____
_____
_____

Knowledge is power make that knowledge yours and you become powerful.

What are the rules when you are actually budgeting for profit?

Never just add ten percent to what you do now!

Make sure that we make a decision based upon intelligent sources of knowledge.

Begin with the end of the mind.

If you are not reviewing your budget often how do you know where you are, where you are going and whether you are on track to get where you want to be?

Have someone else hold you accountable.

Find a quality consultant, a mentor, a coach or an accountant or all of the above!

> Remember, a budget is a plan for your business and ultimately it's all about how much cash you want to end up with.

> Test and measure everything inside your business.

> Make sure you get your books checked and verified by an independent source and if you have been using the same accountant and / or bookkeeper for a long time consider get their figures checked.

Remember it's little things done regularly that makes a big difference.

> Find out what your highest and lowest gross profit margin products and services are.

> Work at what your breakeven point is.

> Work out what your equity and working capital is.

> Generate a ninety day cash flow forecast.

> Create a budget for the next ninety days.

> Take personal responsibility for your profits and financial management in your business, don't abdicate that responsibility to others.

My name is John Millar, I am the Managing Director of More Profit Less Time and I am very grateful for the opportunity that I have had to spend with you today to go through what's a pretty tough subject. I know that if you get your financials under control it will pay dividends in your business and will allow you to generate more profit in less time.
I look forward to seeing you in the next session.

John Millar

Financial Ratios and Quality Indicators

If you monitor the ratios on a regular basis you'll gain insight into how effectively you are managing your business. Lenders also like to evaluate risk by using several sets of ratios; ratios of assets to liabilities, and ratios of lender- investor dollars to owner-investor dollars. Recognize that ratios are indicators and that only you can tell the full story about your business. So the more adapt you are at explaining your financial ratios to your lender, the better she'll understand your business as she makes a credit decision.

LIQUIDITY
Financial ratios in this category measure the company's capacity to pay its debts as they come due.

CURRENT RATIO

Definition:
The ratio between all current assets and all current liabilities; another way of expressing liquidity.

Formula:
- Current assets
- Current Liabilities

Analysis:
- 1:1 current ratio means; the company has $1.00 in current assets to cover each $1.00 in current liabilities. Look for a current ratio above 1:1 and as close to 2:1 as possible.

- One problem with the current ratio is that it ignores timing of cash received and paid out. For example, if all the bills are due this week, and inventory is the only current asset, but won't be sold until the end of the month, the current ratio tells very little about the company's ability to survive.

QUICK RATIO

Definition:
The ratio between all assets quickly convertible into cash and all current liabilities. Specifically excludes inventory.

Formula:
- Cash + accounts Receivable Current Liabilities

Analysis:

- Indicates the extent to which you could pay current liabilities without relying on the sale of inventory — how quickly you can pay your bills. Generally, a ratio of 1:1 is good and indicates you don't have to rely on the sale of inventory to pay the bills.

- Although a little better than the Current ratio, the Quick ratio still ignores timing of receipts and payments.

SAFETY

Indicator of t
he businesses' vulnerability to risk. These ratios are often used by creditors to determine the ability of the business to repay loans.

DEBT TO EQUITY

Definition:
Shows the ratio between capital invested by the owners and the funds provided by lenders.

Formula:
- Debt equity

Analysis:
- Comparison of how much of the business was financed through debt and how much was financed through equity. For this calculation it is common practice to include loans from owners in equity rather than in debt.

- The higher the ratio, the greater the risk to a present or future creditor.

- Look for a debt to equity ratio in the range of 1:1 to 4:1

- Most lenders have credit guidelines and limits for the debt to equity ratio (2:1 is a commonly used limit for small business loans).

- Too much debt can put your business at risk… but too little debt may mean you are not realizing the full potential of your business — and may actually hurt your overall profitability. This is particularly true for larger companies where shareholders want a higher reward (dividend rate) than lenders (interest rate). If you think that you might be in this situation, talk to your accountant or financial advisor.

DEBT COVERAGE RATIO

Definition:
Indicates how well your cash flow covers debt and the capacity of the business to take on additional debt.

Formula:
- Net Profit + Non-cash Expenses Debt

Analysis:

- Shows how much of your cash profits are available to repay debt.
- Lenders look at this ratio to determine if there is adequate cash to make loan payments.
- Most lenders also have limits for the debt coverage ratio.

PROFITABILITY
The ratios in this section measure the ability of the business to make a profit.

SALES GROWTH

Definition:
Percentage increase (or decrease) in sales between two time periods.

Formula:
- Current Year's sales–Last Year's sales Last Year's sales

note: substitute sales for a month or quarter for a shorter term trend.

Analysis:
- Look for a steady increase in sales.
- If overall costs and inflation are on the rise, then you should watch for a related increase in your sales... if not, then this is an indicator that your Prices are not keeping up with your costs.

COGS TO SALES

Definition:
Percentage of sales used to pay for expenses which vary directly with sales.

Formula:
- Cost of goods Sold Sales

Analysis:
Look for a stable ratio as an indicator that the company is controlling its gross margins.

GROSS PROFIT MARGIN

Definition:
Indicator of how much profit is earned on your products without consideration of selling and administration costs.

Formula:

Gross Profit
- Total Sales where gross Profit = Sales less Cost of goods Sold

Analysis:
- Compare to other businesses in the same industry to see if your business is operating as profitably as it should be.

- Look at the trend from month to month. Is it staying the same? Improving? Deteriorating?

- Is there enough gross profit in the business to cover your operating costs?

- Is there a positive gross margin on all your products?

SG&A TO SALES

Definition:
Percentage of selling, general and administrative costs to sales.

Formula:
Selling, general & administrative expenses Sales

Analysis:
- Look for a steady or decreasing percentage indicating that the company is controlling its overhead expenses.

NET PROFIT MARGIN

Definition:
Shows how much profit comes from every dollar of sales.

Formula:
- Net Profit Total Sales

Analysis:
- Compare to other businesses in the same industry to see if your business isoperating as profitably as it should be.
- Look at the trend from month to month. Is it staying the same? Improving? Deteriorating?
- Are you generating enough sales to leave an acceptable profit?
- Trend from month to month can show how well you are managing your operatingor overhead costs.

RETURN ON EQUITY

Definition:
Determines the rate of return on your investment in the business. as an owner or shareholder this is one of the most important ratios as it shows the hard fact about the business — are you making enough of a profit to compensate you for the risk of being in business?

Formula:
- Net Profit equity

Analysis:
- Compare the return on equity to other investment alternatives, such as a savings account, stock or bond.

- Compare your ratio to other businesses in the same or similar industry.

RETURN ON ASSETS

Definition:

Considered a measure of how effectively assets are used to generate a return. (This ratio is not very useful for most businesses.)

Formula:
- Net Profit Total assets

Analysis:
- ROA shows the amount of income for every dollar tied up in assets.

- Year to year trends may be an indicator ... but watch out for changes in the total asset figure as you depreciate your assets (a decrease or increase in the denominator can affect the ratio and doesn't necessarily mean the business is improving or declining.

EFFICIENCY
Also called Asset Management ratio Indicator of how efficiently the company manages its assets.

DAYS IN RECEIVABLES

Definition:
This calculation shows the average number of days it takes to collect your accounts receivable (number of days of sales in receivables).

Formula:
- Average accounts Receivable Sales X 360 days

Analysis:
- Look for trends that indicate a change in your customers' payment habits.

- Compare the calculated days in receivables to your stated terms.

- Compare to industry standards.

- Review an Aging of receivables and be familiar with your customer's payment habits and watch for any changes that might indicate a problem.

ACCOUNTS RECEIVABLE TURNOVER

Definition:
Number of times that trade receivables turnover during the year.
Formula:
Net Sales
Average accounts Receivable

Analysis:
- The higher the turnover, the shorter the time between sales and collecting cash.
- Compare to industry standards.

DAYS IN INVENTORY

Definition:
This calculation shows the average number of days it will take to sell your inventory (number of days sales @ cost in inventory).

Formula:
Average Inventory
Cost of Goods Sold X 360 days

Analysis:
- Look for trends that indicate a change in your inventory levels.
- Compare the calculated days in inventory to your inventory cycle. (Learn how to calculate your inventory cycle in our lesson on Using Financial Statements).
- Compare to industry standards.

INVENTORY TURNOVER

Definition:
Number of times that you turn over (or sell) inventory during the year.

Formula:
- Cost of goods Sold average Inventory

Analysis:
- Generally, a high inventory turnover is an indicator of good inventory management.
- But a high ratio can also mean there is a shortage of inventory.
- A low turnover may indicate overstocking, or obsolete inventory.
- Compare to industry standards.

SALES TO TOTAL ASSETS

Definition:
Indicates how efficiently your business generates sales on each dollar of assets.

Formula:
Sales
Total assets

Analysis:
- A volume indicator that can be used to measure efficiency of your business from year to year.

DAYS IN ACCOUNT PAYABLES

Definition:
This calculation shows the average length of time your trade payables are outstanding before they are paid. (number of days sales @ cost in payables).

Formula:
Average accounts Payable COGS X 360 days

Analysis:
- Look for trends that indicate a change in your payment habits.

- Compare the calculated days in payables to the terms offered by your suppliers.

- Compare to industry standards.

- review an Aging of Payables and be familiar with the terms offered by your suppliers.

ACCOUNTS PAYABLE TURNOVER

Definition:
The number of times trade payables turnover during the year.

Formula:
- COGS
- Average accounts Payable

Analysis:
- The higher the turnover, the shorter the time between purchase and payment.

- A low turnover may indicate that there is a shortage of cash to pay your bills or some other reason for a delay in payment.

Here's an example

7 Steps to More Profit Less Time

Area	Current Figure	Areas of Potential	Increase	New Forecast
# of Enquires	4,000	Host Beneficiary Strategic Alliance, Website SEO, Networking Groups	10%	4,400
Conversion %	25%	Defined USP, Quality Guarantee Sales Training, CRM	10%	27.5%
New Customers	1,000			1,210
Retained Customers	2,000	Members Kit, Newsletters Customer Surveys, Loyalty Program	10%	2,200
Total Customer Base	3,000			3,410
Average $ Sale	$100	Increases Prices, Use a checklist Offer Finance, Upsell and Cross Sell	10%	$110
Average of Transactions	2	Have an engaged database, Sell more consumables, Build a relationship	10%	2.2
Total Revenue	$600,000			$825,220
Average GP Margin %	25%	NO DISCOUNTING, Reduce Waste, Negotiate better trading terms, Measure Everything	10%	27.5%
Total Gross Profit	$150,000			$266,935.20
Fixed Costs	$100,000	Better Time Management, Systemize the routine, Reduce Duplication	10%	$90,000
Net Profit	$50,000			$136,935.50

Now it's your turn!

Keep this page blank for photocopying

Business Essentials Series...

Disc 1 in the Business Essentials Series
Gaining Focus in Your Business
This is about your fundamental learning skills and what you will need to do to change them to vastly improve the way you look
at your development to become a truly effective business owner not just simply remain self-employed.

You will also give you some excellent tools to set goals, work on your plans and create a diary that will allow you to steal your time back to begin moving your business from chaos to control.

Disc 2 in the Business Essentials Series
Getting Your Financials Right
You will learn the importance of understanding your financials.

After all being in business is about making profit and having cash flow work for YOU since you are responsible for your profits.
Become your accountant and book keepers best friend by understanding more about how the financials in your business works so you can ask them better questions to maximise your profits not simply ensure tax compliance.

Disc 3 in the Business Essentials Series
Leveraging Your Business Harder
You will learn the principles of what and how to leverage far more in your business to get more from less and to work far smarter and not just harder.

Here is where you will receive some of the tools you will need to better understand how to get your business flying, what it is you need to test and measure, how to do it and WHY it's so important.

Disc 4 in the Business Essentials Series
How to Generate More Clients Profitably
This is where you will determine your uniqueness, develop a meaningful guarantee and learn the basics of good advertising.

You will gain a better appreciation between the difference of Marketing and Advertising, learn how to get the most for the least investment and ensure that you do it all profitably.

Disc 5 in the Business Essentials Series
Maximising Your Conversion Rates
Get to know how your Sales Pipeline REALLY works and how to identify who your suspects really are, convert prospects into regular shoppers and understand how much more work you can do to maximise your sales experience.

Disc 6 in the Business Essentials Series
Meet and Exceed Your Clients Expectations
Now you have new customers, how do you make sure you KEEP them, how do you wanting to come back time and again while telling their friends? ...this is where you really make a difference.

Disc 7 in the Business Essentials Series
Systemising Your Business For Consistent Excellence
Do you recognise the importance of having systems in your business and how they can improve your profitability?

We show you how to systemise like a corporate while retaining the culture of a smaller business. Understanding how we systemise for routine and humanise for the exceptions will enable you to be the best in your field every time.

Disc 8 in the Business Essentials Series
Do You Have a Champion Team with a Champion Leader?
This is about having the right people on the bus. It starts with you however so you'll learn how to maximise your own skills and then you will attract and retain the right people.

When you understand how the TEAM is the most important part of your business and what needs to be done to achieve the very best from yourselves and others you are well on your way to becoming a better manager of this invaluable resource.

Disc 9 in the Business Essentials Series
The Essentials of Getting Your Time Back.
This is where you get to redefine your time management You will understand better how you can start working far more on the business than in the business than ever before.

You will also finally find out why others can seem to fit more into their day while having a great LIFE – WORK balance (notice the order!)..

Disc 10 in the Business Essentials Series
Simply Brilliant Customer Service.
It's so easy to give mediocre or good customer service but it's just as easy to give amazing service to your customers and delight them.

You will understand the simple easy steps that you must take to provide consistently brilliant service and how to get your team excited about doing it.

Disc 11 in the Business Essentials Series
Discovering DISC and EQ not just IQ.
We believe for things to change first you must change so here you will learn why you behave as you do and just as importantly understand why other people react and act the way they do.

You will also learn what DISC really is and what it isn't. You will learn how to apply these important principles in your recruitment and team management / development.
You will learn how to use these ideas in creating a more dynamic team and discover the what and why of emotional intelligence. You will also develop key strategies for using the knowledge here and the tools we have available on our website and why we place such a massive emphasis on DISC and other tools that support, train and develop your team.
You will also learn how to use these skills and observations at home and socially not just at the workplace.

Disc 12 in the Business Essentials Series
Quality Recruitment.
Recruitment of the right people for the right reasons in the right roles for your team is so incredibly important yet so often ignored or pushed to the rear.

You will learn who the right person is for your business and the role you want filled.

You will be able to identify the right people early in the process to save yourself and them the time and money wasted with antique recruitment methodologies that just don't work anymore.

How to get the best out of your recruitment activities so you can keep the assets you acquire for the long term and get the best return from your investment.

ABOUT THE AUTHOR

John Millar is the Managing Director, Senior Business Coach Trainer and Consultant with More Profit Less Time Pty Ltd and CEO-ONDEMAND. Along with his many other business interests, John is proud to have been an associate of the most successful coaching team in the world.

He is recognized as a global leader and has been benchmarked against over 1,300 colleagues in 31 countries. John has over 25 years of hands-on ownership, management, coaching, and entrepreneurial experience in a broad range of industry sectors, including retail, wholesale, import, export, IT, trades and trade services, automotive, primary production, food services, transport, manufacturing, mining, professional services, the fitness industry, and more.

He has extensive experience developing and providing training for small to medium-sized companies and a variety of publicly listed corporate companies. John is an accomplished and talented public and professional speaker. He has been a mentor working with sales/management activities for businesses with a turnover under $100,000 per annum, over $100 million turnover, and everything in between, with great success.

John currently works with business owners and their teams across Australia and has a "Whatever it takes" attitude that has enabled him to help his clients grow their business profits by up to 800%.

If you are ready to be coached by one of the best in the business, register at:

www.ceo-ondemand.com.au

Make sure to visit www.moreprofitlesstime.com for the new online Management Development Program: The Business Essentials Series.

ACCLAIM FOR JOHN MILLAR'S
Business Coaching and Training in their own words...

"Without John Millar as my Business Coach I wouldn't have a business today."—Grant Jennings Managing Director, Jigsaw Projects

"Taking the decision to be coached and trained by John Millar was carefully considered after experiencing those who over promised and under delivered. I am pleased to say the content of his courses are the tools we all need to master as business owners. His delivery is engaging, thought provoking and empowering and after every session l came away re-energised. John always makes himself available for business building advice both via Skype and face to face beyond the scope of delivery. With his extensive personal experience in building small businesses, he knows and understands what it takes to establish and grow a business.I have no hesitation endorsing John Millar as an educator and business coach and the bonus is he is a very nice person."—Anne Lederman Managing Director FB Salons"

Johns training with my management team was excellent, it was very different from the business coaching and support I have had in the past. John was clear, thoughtful and he addressed the issues we needed to cover without us even knowing they were being addressed! His follow up has been fantastic and exactly what I needed. I would recommend John and his team to anyone looking at getting some business coaching and training done" —Wendy Crawford, Peopleworx

"In my dealings with John as our business coach, I have found him to be a motivated and insightful agent of positive change. He is able to burrow down to the root cause of issues and introduce effective forms of measurement. John then identifies and implements practical solutions and is there to provide the gentle persuasion required to ensure that results are achieved." —Mark Felton, Lindale Insurances

"You have coached and trained us so well throughout the year that we are now used to & find it easy to prepare a 90 day plan, then breaks it down to actionable bite size pieces. Planning in business & personal life certainly is important. It allows us to identify the important things & the bigger picture. Thank you for your support & guidance throughout the year. And not to mention your insight, external perspective to review & assist our business moving forward." —Linda Turner, Director Roy A McDonald Certified Practicing Accountants

"If you want to achieve sales results you never thought were possible and give yourself a competitive edge my strong suggestion is to engage John services and listen closely to what John has to say, during the time I was trained by John I was one of eight sales consultants in a national business for 10 out of the 13 months I lead the sales tally and in 1 quarter I generated three times the revenue of the national sales force combined. Johns training and experience was well worth the investment and paid big dividends. Thanks John." —Julian Fadini, Bellvue Capital

"John is a very enthusiastic trainer and business coach, he is very passionate about getting business owners and their team where they need to be. He goes the extra mile to keep ahead of the latest developments which he then uses to benefit his clients." —Darren Reddy CPA

"I have been to a few seminars and heard John speak numerous times about sales, marketing and business. He is a very knowledgable and extremely enthusiastic business coach in all his interactions and I would recommend him to all business owners who need a sales and marketing boost!" —Andrew Heath, Managing Director, Fresh Living Group

"I worked with John Millar and found his business knowledge, passion and innovation to be inspiring. He has always been able to set (and achieve) strategic long and short-term goals both for himself and his clients without losing that personal connection he builds with everyone he meets. He has been and I believe will continue to be a strong mentor and trainer for anyone wanting to take that next step in their business." —Bree Webster, Online Marketing Guru

"Massive Action Day" – what an understatement, John Millars 4 hour frenzy challenged me to seriously review areas of my business I would not have gone to …. In this way, the process identified incongruence's in my mind, my business and my modus operandi. It's created a paradigm shift. Thanks John, the road map just got a whole lot clearer. Your friendship and insights since 2003 have been a gift to my business and I." —Andrew Reay, Counsellor, Hypnotherapist and Counsellor, Thinkshift Transformations

"John Millar is not your usual Business coach or trainer; he gets involved with you and your business and provides hands on help to make sure you follow through on his advice. He is highly motivated to help his clients and his personal guarantee certainly shows this. He has now transposed his thoughts, advice and love of good business onto a series of DVD's in his business venture – More Profit Less Time. This has excellent tips and advice for anyone either starting out or already in business. I highly recommend John to any business owner who wants to run a business and not a j.o.b.!" —Darren Cassidy, Managing Director HR2U

"I and many of my Business Partners and colleagues have worked with John since 2010 as our business oath, trainer and motivator and found him to be an extremely motivational person to assist us achieve our business goals. This company and its products allows for John's skill set to be accessed by a wider number of potential clients. His very professional DVD series is extremely good value for money and is easily accessible for all of us who are time poor. If you are looking to maximise your and your business's results and to start achieving your goals and dreams, contact John; you won't look back!!" —Mark Cleland, Mortgage Choice

"John develops real relationships with the people he comes into contact with. He is pasionate about what he does. His DVD and group training series, is full of good ideas and process to make your business better. Knowing what to do and actually doing it are two different things. John is excellent at helping you get things done." —Carey Rudd, Sales Director, Online Knowledge

"I have known John since 2004 and found him to be extremely knowledgably in both Sales and Business systems as a business coach without peer. John has provided me with business advice as well as personal coaching over the years, helping me with the running of my organisation. I'm impressed with John's DVD series where he has condensed a lot of the information in an easy to follow format that any business owner can use immediately. I wish he had released these DVDs earlier, as they are a goldmine of information, and practical how to that allow anyone to increase the profit in their business and get back valuable wasted time." —Steve Psaradellis, Managing Director, TEBA

"John's DVD and workbook delivery of his no-nonsense advice provides a low-cost option for those business owners looking to set and achieve goals that will increase profit. I found the conversational style of the DVD's easy to follow, whilst the requirement to pause the DVD and write down some action points ensured a level of commitment to the advice being provided." — Mark Felton, Lindale Insurances

"I only met John briefly at a BNI meeting and knew instantly i need to hire him for my business as my business coach. His attitude towards work and how to improve my cash line had an instant effect on before, even before I finally hired him on an official basis. I found myself thinking "what would John do" and this was only after just meeting him. I cannot see my business expend and give me "More Profit Less Time" without John's expert direction and training. If you want to succeed in business life, you need John Millar, without him you're just kidding yourself " —Leslie Cachia, Managing Director, Letac Drafting

"I can highly recommend John Millar to any business owner who wants to grow his business. When I hear very positive feedback from colleagues who are skeptics by nature about John's ability and skills, I know John will help all those he comes in contact with. John comes with a selfless nature and the willingness to work inside a client's business to make it succeed. Rare indeed!" —Darren Cassidy, Managing Director, HR2U"I first met John Millar in mid-2010 and have always found him to be of an honest and generous character that engenders an easy association with him. I love how easy he is to listen to and how passionate he is about his work and topics. John demonstrates a love for life and his work and I have no hesitation in recommending his services." —Kathie M Thomas, Managing Director, VA

"I have listened to John speak on a number of occasions and find him a very knowledgeable speaker with a passion for what he does. I have also interacted with a number of his clients and they all tell me that he helps them achieve results in their business. If you are looking for business help John is a person you can trust." —Carey Rudd, Sales Director, Online Knowledge

"John knows his stuff, he knows how the get results, John has so many great ideas in building a business and helping business owners work less and make more money. John has released a DVD set on doing just that. I have watched the 1st one and it was great, very informative and easy to understand, I happily recommend John to anyone in need of help and guidance" —Frank Eramo, Proprietor, Dynotune

"I have known John only for a short time, however the impact that he has had on me, not just my business has helped me to visualise opportunities that I began to doubt my ability to realise. He is encouraging and at the same time challenging so that he can/you can, begin to see how to maximise the business potential, John calls it being an unreasonable friend, I call it being a mate. If you have any questions about the direction of your business, if you want to seem your bottom line improve not just turnover but real profit, if you want a person who will work with you then I strongly recommend that you engage him at your earliest convenience. John is the best thing that has happened to my business. I could tell you about the way he is on track to make 1/2 a million for me on his contacts alone, but that actually sells him short, he has become like my partner in business, and cares about my success as if it was his own, we will flourish because I took the step to employ his training to help me grow. If you get a chance to get him training you, don't wait like I did, get in as quickly as possible, his time is your business and if like me your business is to make money, then every day you don't have him on retainer you lose money." —Russell Summers,

Managing Director, The Give Life Centre

"It's usually easy to be mediocre in business but it's impossible when you have John Millar training you. He has been my right hand since 2003!" —David Manser, CFO, Hydrosteer

"I now have a commercial, profitable business and now it's my choice when I work IN my business and when I work ON it and have had john helping me in business since 1988. I can't imagine not having John as a part of our business." —David Wall, Director, D&K Transport

"The work John has done since 2008 coaching and training our marketing team, administration and finance teams, buyers, store managers and staff nationally have been fantastic." —Ross Sudano, Director, Anaconda Adventure Stores

"John is a creative, professional, practical and committed business coach and trainer. His approach since we first met him in 1994 to working with a client team through the application of useful tools, information and anecdotes along with his easy going & easy to understand delivery sets him apart from other business coaches that I have used in the past." —Anthony Beasley, Director, The Astra Group

"I have worked with John Millar for the since 2004 and I didn't think it was possible to achieve what we have achieved together. His business coaching, training and services just get better and better!" —Terrance Chong, Managing Director, Echo Graphics and Printing

"John's business coaching, training and support has transformed our business across Australia and New Zealand since 2008."—Rose Vis, Managing Director, VIP Australia

"We first met John in 2005, he is AMAZING at sales, marketing, operations, logistics, finance training and so much more. Since engaging John as our business coach our business has exploded, our team are happy, our clients are raving about us and my husband and I now take at least 12 weeks holidays a year, EVERY year." —Shirley Du, Director, Goldline Technology

"It's the no nonsense results driven business coaching and training focus John bought to the table that had such a massive effect on our business." —David Runkel, Director, Tracomp Fabrication and Steel

"We started working with John in early 2010, within 90 days of working with and being trained by John Millar we had the biggest and most profitable month in our 15 year history. That's impressive." —Hugh Gilchrist, Managing Director, Australian Moulding Company

"If you don't have John as your business trainer you aren't meeting your business potential." —Don Robertson, Director, Medallion Electrical Services

Thank You!

www.ingramcontent.com/pod-product-compliance
Lightning Source LLC
Chambersburg PA
CBHW050806180526
45159CB00004B/1571